Night Court
Erica Goss

Glass Lyre Press

Copyright © 2017 Erica Goss
Paperback ISBN: 978-1-941783-34-4

All rights reserved: except for the purpose of quoting brief passages for review, no part of this book may be reproduced or transmitted in any form or by any means, electronic or mechanical, including photocopying, recording, or by any information storage and retrieval system, without permission in writing from the publisher.

Cover art: © Sebastian Schubanz | Dreamstime.com
Design & layout: Steven Asmussen
Copyediting: Linda E. Kim

Glass Lyre Press, LLC
P.O. Box 2693
Glenview, IL 60025
www.GlassLyrePress.com

CONTENTS

Acknowledgments ix

I

Encontrada	13
Act Normal	14
The Art of Negotiation	15
2:00 AM	16
What Insomniacs Hear	17
Fire Season	18
Ghost Hive	19
Answer the Phone	20
Omens	21
Often	22
Night Court	23

II

Remember Three Words	27
My Beautiful Mother Opens Her Mouth	29
Scraps	30
At Thirteen I Let a Boy Shoot My Dog With a BB Gun	31

II (CON'T)

The Art of Smoking	32
Noche	33
Strange Land	34
Conception	35
Phase	36
Salt to Salt	37
My Father at Seventy	39
Post-Last Rites	40

III

This Cold Devotion	43
The White Bear	45
The Art of Leaving	47
Closer	49
Flight 805	50
Back to Empty	51
The Finding Spot	52
Visiting Hours	53
The Appointment	54
Arrhythmia	55

IV

Acquired Taste	59
Easter Sunday	60
Boden	62
The Art of Demolition	63
Cover	64
No Humble Fruit	65
Theobroma Cacao	66
Camellia Garden in October	67
Like the Man Who Fell In Love With Jesus	68
Afternoon in the Shape of a Pear	69
Irresistible	70
Shiver	71
While You Can	72
Seduction of the Bee Queen	73
The Redwoods	74
This is a Wild Place	75

V

Love Poem with Broken Things	79
Early Morning, San Bernardino, 1969	80
I Am No Falconress	81
Blindsided	82
In The Fairytale Forest	83
Photographs of Elderly Poets	84

for Don

Acknowledgments

I am grateful to the editors of the publications in which many of these poems first appeared, sometimes in earlier or differently-titled versions:

Bone Bouquet: "Fire Season"; *Bryant Literary Review*: "Like the Man Who Fell in Love With Jesus," "Noche"; *Café Review*: "This is a Wild Place"; *Canary*: "Ghost Hive"; *Catamaran*: "Encontrada"; *Caveat Lector*: "While You Can"; *Chantarelle's Notebook*: "The Redwoods," "Often"; *Comstock Review*: "Acquired Taste," "The Art of Negotiation," "Back to Empty"; *Contrary*: "Early Morning, San Bernardino, 1969", "I Am No Falconress", "In the Fairytale Forest"; *Eclectica*: "Strange Land", "Love Poem with Broken Things", "The Art of Smoking"; *Escape Into Life*: "Arrhythmia"; *Hazmat*: "Conception"; *Hummingbird Review*: "Boden", "Salt to Salt"; *Innisfree*: "Scraps"; *Lake Effect*: "Night Court"; *Leaf By Leaf*: "What Insomniacs Hear"; *Main Street Rag*: "Act Normal", "My Beautiful Mother Opens Her Mouth", "This Cold Devotion"; *Passager*: "Phase"; *Penwood Review*: "Camellia Garden in October"; *Pentimento*: "Visiting Hours"; *Perigee*: "Answer the Phone"; *Red Rock Review*: "Flight 805"; *Reed*: "The Art of Leaving"; *Sand Hill Review*: "Irresistible", "At Thirteen I let a Boy Shoot My Dog With a BB Gun," "Remember Three Words"; *Santa Clara Review*: "Afternoon in the Shape of a Pear"; *San Francisco Peace & Hope*: "Shiver", "The Art of Demolition", "The Finding Spot"; *Stirring*: "Cover", "Omens"; *The Bohemian*: "My Father at Seventy"; *The Bohemian Journal*: "White Bear"; *The Lake*: "Photographs of Elderly Poets"; *The Tishman Review*: "Post-Last Rites"; *Tiger's Eye*: "The Appointment"; *Up the Staircase*: "Theobroma Cacao"; *Zoland Poetry Journal*: "Easter Sunday."

Several of these poems appeared in *Wild Place*, 2012, Finishing Line Press.

Thanks to *Many Mountains Moving*, who chose "2:00 a.m." as the winning poem for 2011. Thanks also to the *Comstock Review* for awarding Special Merit to "The Art of Negotiation," to *Reed Magazine* for awarding "The Art of Leaving" the Edwin Markham Poetry Prize, to the Soul-Making Keats Contest for giving Second Place to "Encontrada," and to *Passager* for awarding "Phase" Honorable Mention.

I am indebted to Jeannine Hall Gailey and Kelly Davio for their guidance with this manuscript. Thanks also to the members of the Brown Bag Poetry Workshop, whose creativity and faithfulness inspire me.

I

Encontrada

I have never learned to wander
to trust in grass and stars and mouthfuls of air.

If I ramble without keys or shoes
I might meet my ghosts, who always seem friendly

at first. No drifting allowed, no matter the delicious
temptation of the vanishing point. I'd rather hit

a sign than turn an unnamed corner
regardless of its lonesome beauty. And so I study

maps of the world, avoiding
shady groves hung with moss,

or streets tense with empty cars
or large bodies of water. When lost

they say, keep to one spot.
Don't meander. That's how you found me

a map of the spirits stuffed in my back pocket.
All I had to do was stay put.

Act Normal

Little dark country:
my dictatorship of one.
I am detained here night after night,
denied visitors while deficits mount
and markets crash.

Outside this humid room
the forest edges closer.
Its silence is white noise
against a black sky.

See what speaking out gets you:
bruised limbs, the bloody floor –
bed like a hot sidewalk.
This is not the time to ponder
what might happen to me.
It's always best to act normal.

Don't talk about the boxes
stuffed with your dreams
bobbing somewhere in the Pacific.

Never let on about the damp walls
lined with photographs of the Disappeared.
Dictators merge with spectators
until they all look the same
stepping backward through the gallery.
The mothers stand outside in the long twilight,
cupping their hands around the cold air
that rises from Earth.

Someone, somewhere
holds my picture up.
My body opens to the night.

The Art of Negotiation

The fairies know about trades.
They don't ask for money, land or fame.
They want a voice, a lock of hair,

an invitation to the party,
to eat from the prince's plate.

They circle the bed
just after the moon sets,
making offers:

for a few minutes of sleep,
some herbs from the garden;
for an hour, my little dog;
for a whole night,
they really need
my two strong young sons.
Bringing on sleep is not easy,
and I'm a particularly hard case.

Cut my herbs, I tell them – the more you take,
the better they grow;
my little dog will soon
return to me.
But I am not so broken
nor so deprived, to trade
my children for magic.

Not yet, the fairies reply – but after
a week, black holes open
before you. After a month,

shadows take human shape.
No one lasts a year.
No one.

2:00 AM

Sleep ends, percussive, final. I don't speak,
try not to think, but sometimes

I just need a good story. Once,
a woman asked twenty-five Catholics what they thought

Heaven would be like. She got twenty-five different
answers. When my husband was a boy,

he broke a flask of holy water.
The glass cut through his small hand,

lodged in the bone, leaving a Y-shaped scar
thick as rope. The night, ribbed like corduroy,

leaves marks on my skin. No one calls me,
no child cries. Why this vigilance?

I rub my cheek against the night. Heaven
is one enormous national park. It smells like

childhood. The prince waits patiently until
Sleeping Beauty wakes, even if it takes

a hundred years. I kiss my pillow.

What Insomniacs Hear

The clatter of souls
entering new bodies

thumping hurtle of an emergency vehicle:
fluorescent bubble, full speed ahead

frogs and crickets
whose shrill demands for love
sift through the lead-lidded hours

telepathy of dogs
across backyards

tree roots forcing up
suburban sidewalks

autumn's held breath
winter's all-night parties
spring's lizard stealth
summer's continuous shout

short gasps, whistles
air chunked by windmills,
water pumping up and down hills

the sea as it dilates across the sand
reaches the cliffs, falls back

the murmuring circle of heads
that hovers between me
and sleep

sigh of theater seats
as a small, disheveled audience
settles in for the late-night movie:
my dreams on the screen.

Fire Season

Whatever we were
looking for is gone:

the door we saw in a dream,
instructions for time travel,

poles tacked with posters
of the missing.

The aroma of houses dying
two hundred miles away
rises into the troposphere,

as television screens explode,
ending a million cop shows.

Call it summer, if you must
but I know its true name,
caramel skies and edgy refrain

and strange delicacies:
marrow forced from split bones,

fog billowing through
silent trees like a last hope,

and when the sky clears
the whittled neighborhoods: row
after row of chimneys.

Ghost Hive

After colony collapse disorder surfaced around 2005, the losses approached one-third of all bees, despite beekeepers' best efforts to ensure their health.
—New York Times, 3/28/13

If they were dead
we could understand it:

compound eyes gone flat
abdomens dry and crisp

but they vanished
like the pictures I made as a child

like my imaginary friends
like my father – gone,

as if there was nothing
left between us – gone,

like sweetness
fading from the mouth

leaving us with nothing to mourn
and no one to punish –

we clean the hive
again.

Answer the Phone

Before, the dead sent letters
sheets of tissue so thin

a hand passed through them like smoke.
They dried the tongue like warm red wine,

glittered our dreams into fragments.

Now the dead use the phone like everyone else;
they ring once and wait. We press the receiver

to our ears, hear the long static hum,

faint clicks and breaths,
explanations and descriptions. They want one

thing only, to tell us what they saw
when one light went out

and another turned on. We want to
show them the pictures we've taken

since they left us: that cathedral in central Europe;
the jellyfish at a California aquarium.

We forget what we needed to tell the dead
as we rush too quickly from sleep.

Their letters stopped coming years ago.

We wait by the phone.

OMENS

Tap of bone on glass —
a clue, some chill intelligence.

Morning unfolds a series of warnings:
truncated telephone rings,
the cello's long vibration.

When the call comes that he is gone
you see the links
in the day's secret systems.

You begin to make preparations
some kind of plan for the future
as if the thing could be put right;

as if the walls of your house
had not just burst open.

Often

When I am alone
the wind comes up suddenly
as if to remind me
of all I fear;

doors tilt on their hinges
and crumpled lists
scuttle sideways
across the floor

but I pretend the wind
is the harmless burp
of the dishwasher
or the dryer rolling its damp wheel;

and if, in spite of the noises
of innocent appliances
I still think about death
it's never my own:

my list of losses is long
and orderly: at the end
I'm left alone and the wind
comes up suddenly.

Night Court

After midnight
when the rates are cheapest
I put my tragedies on the witness stand.
How fresh and alive

they become
one by one
permanent and hard
as jewels.

They do not flinch
when I question them.
They have sworn to tell the truth
and nothing else.

I test them again and again:
they are precise as nightmares
and I am never more awake.
If there is no safe place

at least this night court has rules:
I know all of the answers
in advance. This, my examination,
my handbook on how to live.

II

REMEMBER THREE WORDS

Apple, penny, table. I've lost
the right lens from my glasses.
Draw a house. We lived across
the street from the library.
I got my library card when
I was five. What time is it?
I could check out as many
books as I wanted. And
God knows I wanted. More
than I could carry.
What month is it? I crossed
the street, holding hands
with my sister. Came home
after two years at Holy Names.
Got married at nineteen.
Count aloud backwards
from 20 to 1. Two teenagers
and a baby in diapers. Jim
Beam was my best friend.
Burned all of my diaries.
Say the months of the year
in reverse order. A twelve-
year-old boy killed my brother.
He was nineteen. My mother
told the killer's mother: we both
lost a son today. How is
your mood today? Of course
my sister is already out
of the hospital. She always
has to be first. Draw a clock
at 11:05. In other words,
the people in here have
no class. No, I don't want
any water. In other words,
you don't have to shout.

Do you remember the
three words? Better, worse,
the same.

My Beautiful Mother Opens Her Mouth

My beautiful mother opens her mouth
rods hold her teeth together
when she yawns her jaw clicks

she touches cologne to each wrist
and the soft veins inside her elbows

stepping off a plane she clutches me
her little piece of home
inhales smog like hit of dope

she watches the sun set over LA
and sees what a reverence for size
can do to a place

my beautiful mother has smooth oily skin
her eyes reflect light like shields

our house smells like rust and sweat
and something else

some days my beautiful mother lies
on her back in bed and closes her eyes
ich sterbe*, she says over and over

people at the grocery store stare
my beautiful mother pushes the shopping cart
in the center of the aisle

someday she will miss winter
but for now this calm is bought
and paid for

*"I'm dying"

Scraps

When I was seven, food I threw away
reappeared on my plate each day until I ate it,
blubbering, licking tears

from the corners of my mouth. She had a hunger,
has it still, for green potatoes, rubbery turnips,
apples bitten past the seeds.

Dried cheese rinds, cold cups of tea,
and morsels of bread, always bread
littered the kitchen counters of my childhood.

If only I had understood their power,
her crude magic. In the war the neighbors
called her Hamster for her talent.

She scoured torn streets with her little bag
while her mother and sisters lay quietly starving.
"Bitte geehrter Herr, kann ich den haben?"*

At seventeen I drove until I lost sight of her
and flung my lunch from the blue Toyota, watched
it burst open, orange rolling away from the dented

sandwich, the small box of raisins intact.
I did not see her pick up scraps of paper bag
and wet bread hours later.

Had I only known,
I might have been a better daughter.
I might still be her child.

*"Please, sir, may I have that?"

At Thirteen I Let a Boy Shoot My Dog With a BB Gun

A little older than
me he rumbled out
a laugh in his newly
acquired man-
voice the gun a sexy
toy we barely understood
the dog yelped stumbled
breath coming fast a hard
lump rising next
to his tail his name
was Happy he did not walk
for a week he ate
my socks and chomped
lizards from the air
the boy had sly brown
eyes and a moustache-
in-training I don't remember
his name to touch him
to place my hand below
his flat white stomach
I would have done
much worse things

The Art of Smoking

It's best to start young. Suck up
secondhand smoke. Notice
how careless adults are. Sneak

a puff while their backs are turned, while
your grandmother brews another pot
of Maxwell House. At twelve finish

your first cigarette, down to the filter.
Squelch the urge to vomit. At fifteen
discover menthols. Hang out

in the smoking grounds at high school.
Snap your jaw to make rings. Light up
right in front of your mother. Blow

smoke out your bedroom window. Play
games where you try to go a whole day
without one. Relish the ache

that floods your body. Try to quit.
Crumple the crush-proof box and let
the tobacco drift through the air

like confetti. Buy a new pack
one hour later. Inhale and stagger
around the room. At twenty-two

visit your grandmother in the hospital.
Forget to eat. Grow thinner and thinner.
When she dies, smoke more.

Noche

Once in Mulege, Jose's father drove me back
to the long beach coated with moonlight.

Fish lingered in black water, suspended on
their plastic bones. The boat rocked slowly,

chipping blue paint into the swells. Two naked
boys floated by in a canoe, laughing quietly.

At sunset, fishermen had pulled a turtle from the sea
and lain her on her back. She took three hours to die,

flippers tracing circles in the air. Jose's
father let me out and drove back to town.

I sat in the cool sand and stared at
the charcoal outlines of mountains.

Turtle meat is pearl colored. It leaves
a film of oil inside the mouth.

All night the taste of the sea rolled
over my tongue. When the moon set

I saw star after star
streak the dark with white fire.

Strange Land

Wind brings
the American desert
to our front door

inside the house
it's the old country

America takes practice
mother prepares
our daily lessons

each morning we emigrate
our fermenting lunchboxes
ripe with foreign stink

the war of two languages
leaves us mute in school
speak up, the teacher says

red ants pierce the heart
of our flimsy suburb
slip into bags of sugar

paper wasps ping the house
build nests from wood
and their own fierce saliva

the insatiable wind
presses against the walls
America drifts under the doorsill

mother scrubs the hot windows
scans the hazy air
always look up, she says

how did she outlast her childhood
in a black cellar
while bombers inked the sky?

Conception

My mother leans back
against the river stones.
Above her the sky is a vast
room she remembers

from childhood. She thinks
of flying, of crossing the ocean.
There is a man whose face
swims in a swirl of words.

My mother looks up,
her body's plan clear to her now.
There are debts to be paid,
and hard days coming.

Everything has been taken.
My mother closes her hand
around a river stone.
Her eyes are open.

Phase

It started in the morning,
when my father's heart wobbled
like the eccentric moon.

The doctors, wiser than they looked,
refused my blood offer.

Spinning away from me
he landed on a bed
as wide and empty
as a lunar sea.

All that pale afternoon
I listened to the deep space
sounds of the hospital.

At 4:00, my father sat up, scattering
blankets and trays, sending
instruments into panicked
stacks of red lights,

swung his numb legs
off the bed, and I

felt the weight of things falling,
a hammer, a feather,
waves and my own blood,
which I could not give away.

Salt to Salt

1.

At the lip of the Pacific
a shoe fills with sand.
It's a huge shoe, a man's shoe,
the size my father used to wear,

mass-produced in a country where
the people have small hands and feet.
Now it rocks in front of me
dilapidated, saturated

as the sea pulls boots of silt
up past my ankle bones. Maybe
I should let the beach absorb me

wait until the sand closes
over my head
while a sea lion regards me
with one innocent, chocolate eye.

2.

We dwell inside each other, salt to salt
yet the sea and I are strangers, opaque
as parents to their children.

Dead below the knees
my father watched continents drift
in and out of view
those big feet in lopsided running shoes.

In the end he forgot everything
lost in that seductive vista:

islands, hazy peaks,
the water's sliding surfaces.

      3.

We are not finished –

a lone shoe
is the punchline to
some impenetrable joke

and me at the water's edge
ready for more uncanny gifts.

My Father at Seventy

In the warm shallows of summer nights
my father walks with coyotes.

In the hours when the sleep I've chased finally arrives
he hears them, yipping in the distance

and he rises, pulls on his boots and tramps
outside the breezy tall-ceilinged house

where he lives alone in the Chinese village along
the Sacramento River.

They don't bother him, he says,
but there is something about the way

their voices get louder as he walks in the moonlight
along the levee, louder

and then softer, fading away when he stops.
At home they find their way into his dreams,

green eyes arranged in untidy rows,
shaggy dog-heads

Outlined in gray against the black night.
My father, open-eyed on his

bed in the deep summer quiet
remembers the coyote

almost forty years past, the one he shot
to protect my little brother and me,

one charmed summer.

Post-Last Rites

I wake the compost
from its slumber,
break and pierce it
with my shovel.

It steams at me,
releasing scents of
last year's rain. I pull
the pile apart, press

my hand into the living
warmth, drop chopped
stems and petals
of funeral flowers

into last year's salads,
green beans, corn cobs,
newspaper headlines.
I work the shovel

corner to corner, move
dry edges to the center,
cover the flowers
in soft damp layers.

A shimmer
of flies, fragile wings
catching the sun.

III

This Cold Devotion

> Teach me how to shed / this cold devotion /by which memory / is exchanged for alertness.
>
> —Tess Gallagher, "Lynx Light"

What if I died right here?
you ask, pulsing out a slow finale
gaze focused
and feral

you want an answer

      if I understand correctly
you have volunteered to die first
leaving me to explain
the naked man in my bed
to the police
who will
no doubt
ask a lot of questions

      my father, who was not known
for his ability to plan
ended his life on a dirt road
children
found him days later
arms wrapped around his shriveling legs
bare white feet, yellow toenails
gripping the earth
      children who see a dead man
carry the memory like a handful of shrapnel

      did they tap him on the shoulder
do other kids taunt them now:
you touched the dead guy by the creek…
does my father's death divide their lives

into before and after
like it does mine

        if you died right here I would drop my ear
to the silence of your stopped heart and lungs
breathe in the denim, cut grass scents of your skin
kiss your eyelids shut
feel you shrink out of my body
one last time
and then
only then
reach for the phone

The White Bear

A man came and lay down beside her, and behold it was the White Bear, who cast off the form of a beast during the night.

—The Blue Fairy Book

Too young for regrets or suspicion
I climbed his thick body

watched one paw lap over the other
claws tilted inward as I held on
and we swayed down the road.

Back home mama and the children
stared at the dirt floor. Papa counted
pieces of gold.

I walked away from my childhood,
little breasts a surprise on my chest.

What would love be like?
Mama and papa: rustling, a groan.
Seven children among the dented pots.

Each night I put out the light. Only then
did he come to me, pull back the furs
and slide his hands up my arms,

the hands of a prince:
calloused from the sword
and the grip of his fingertips.

Our bed burned those Nordic nights.
Days were empty and twilit. Still a child

I listened for his breathing, tilted the candle
over his noble head. Now
I go begging from door to door

looking for him in cities, in men's faces
our pale baby strapped to my back
her hair like the snow

that piled up outside the long hall
corners dwindled
and dark with enchantment.

The Art of Leaving

She loved a tall man with eyes like
old green bottles,
a coughing laugh and an unsweetened smile.

Cruelty was his mother tongue.
As a boy he bathed
his wounds in bowls of cold soup.

The sun shone on him like it does in California,
in late winter,
careful like museum lights angled

to illuminate a painting while
the wall behind
recedes into darkness.

Expert in the art of offense,
he never learned
defense. He took it out on the telephone,

splintered against a wall, on the garbage can
rolling forlorn
down the suburban street.

The children watched him through book covers,
watched her sprinkle
cocoa on her morning oatmeal.

She skimmed and skimmed but finally
one day the fat
was gone. She had no choice but

to cut into the flesh, scrape the bones clean,
pack them neatly
and flee. How they rattled in her suitcase,

those bones shiny with wear, pitted with
disease, dust of
old wars, and new ones yet to come.

Closer

A mountain looks simple
from a distance

the way a marriage looks simple
from a distance:

two people, children, a dog;
silence, slopes, a peak.

I climbed a mountain.
I entered the house.

Spider webs hang in every room,
persistent little habitats

of home economics.
Outside, they bend and flow

with the movements of air
like the hammocks we hung

and never lay in. Fault lines,
goldmines, children and parents

lost from each other:
what should be orderly falls apart.

We are tenants here for a short time
and for a short time the windows

of our house reflect the evening light
as night grows closer.

Flight 805
Detroit to Minneapolis

You invent a life of straight lines
        and wide, gentle curves.
                Tiny houses, red mailboxes,

and snowy yards mean nothing.
        Watch their letters
                pass through clouds. Again

you find yourself wedged
        between strangers. How
                often have you searched

this country above your head: sky
        with its private cities, rippled floor
                and sudden gaps? Try

to fit it into the box of your camera;
        even a child knows better. Still
                the sensation:

floating out of your body, as if to enter
        the landscape glimpsed
                from the window. Know

the wind, how it presses from all sides,
        how thin the skin between you
                and the cold. Soon

you breathe thick air at sea level,
        and the sky comes all the way
                down to the ground.

Back to Empty

Softened bones, an offering
but *how* stayed just beyond my comprehension.

A woman bumping into doors,
my stomach introduced herself.

Stretch and snap of latex.
People pushing fingers into me.

I clenched and smiled at strangers,
savored our discomfort. When

my child was born
the world contracted one last time with

all its unknown faces
and I spent a long day shrinking,

pulled back to empty,
clean.

The Finding Spot

Piled beneath
the willows, human stash
this small wet evening

infant girls accumulate
like autumn leaves
and this will be

the finding spot
they talk about when asked
where they were born

oh to be wanted
here is where she rested
she was poor, she had

the smell of village cooking
in her hair
there was a note

but she could not read or write
girls are not allowed
to learn

some will stay in China
some will go to America
or Canada or Spain

some return
to the grass
in little boxes

Visiting Hours

You don't panic when you see him
sitting at the window of his private room

where he's been sketching a bottle of hand lotion.
Something else sets in, let's call it pre-panic,

like the first time he left you, dropped your hand
and stepped through the kindergarten door

or when you left him in a dorm
with two wall-eyed roommates.

This not-quite-panic, this warmup-for-panic
served you well when he called you from

the highway with a crumpled fender.
You made him call the tow truck, made him

take responsibility, for once,
smug and parental and not panicking.

But when he looks through you, tells you about *movie night*
and *occupational therapy*

shows you the ten pills a day he needs
just to keep his world horizontal

you let the clean heat of panic constrict your heart,
loosen your gut, the sweat rolling down your scalp

like the first rain after summer's drought
in a California meadow.

The Appointment

I sit with the other parents,
come to hear the facts. Our
unborn children bear labels:
irregular, anomalous, damaged.

Like threatened bees, passing
signals between antennae,
mothers and fathers hand
each other pamphlets.

How large their eyes seem,
their mouths working around
unpronounceable maladies
and unthinkable costs.

They keep their voices low
as if a baby slept nearby
or funeral was happening
in the next room.

Arrhythmia

No doctor can explain
the irregular, cavorting pulse
of my son's heart,
its refusal to beat
like other hearts.
It writes in spikes
of code rolling
across graph paper,
telling us about
the lion and the lamb
that live in his chest.
And so he carries
the mystery of his heart
like a visitor from the future
where people understand
its off-beat rhythm,
a heart ahead of its time.

IV

vi

Acquired Taste

My tongue seeks trouble,
chafe of grinding stone,
what's swept away: the
bitter discards.

My tongue wants to leave
sweetness behind
like childhood. No more
mindless syrup blunting
raw edges,

no more disguising things
with bland counterparts.

Melt off the candy coating
and give me my medicine
straight. My tongue wants

the unsweetened life,
bread of rough grains and grit,
hard muscle of a fish
swimming upstream.

Easter Sunday

Joy comes, grief goes, we know not how
    —James Russell Lowell

    1.

After a rigid winter
with too many days
spent in classrooms,
the faint presence of birds
disturbs the windowsills.

Trees open their mouths,
fine-cut leaves cup air —
careful, the way a woman

slides a hand beneath
her child's oval
skull and lifts
his face to hers.

    2.

I have been too loyal
to grief. I have
given corners to darkness,
allowed myself
to think love shrinks, cold.
Now when sorrow answers
it doesn't matter.
I tell my own stories,

place colored eggs
under shrubs, behind stones,
coddle a few in a flowerpot.
One by one, children
take them back,

heads tempera bulbs
in morning's convocation.
Joy scrambles sadness. Lord,
break this day over my head.
Light sticks to me like yolk.

Boden

I know it's hard to love me;
crushed under cities
scraped from your shoes.

I want attention. I want
to live under fingernails
find my way into your mouth.

I give you monkey-flower, nettles,
the bay tree's rising scent.
I understand sacrament.

Spread a blanket over me.
I banish isolation.
Take your lover right here.

Clotted within me,
the dead are silent.
I could rouse them, but I won't.

I lift mountains over bones.
In the green grass of the field
take your rest in me.

The Art of Demolition

Men built me
while other men imagined
my pieces on the ground.

I think I know who's winning.
All of the rooms in my heart
collapse.

A wave starts on one side
then windows vibrate like teeth
under the drill.

My structures shift
in strategic chunks
towers drop like obedient trees

just before I hit the street.
My corners stretch
like arms folding a sheet.

Particles of me settle in the lungs:
immortal,
walking forward.

Cover

What a relief
to accept this interruption,
stand at the window

where a Canadian storm
writes its last chapter
in black and white.

Snow: a surface that tempts
disturbance – yet each crystal
hides a secret sting.

The garden, updated with new skin,
enlarges from this
unexpected gift.

You forget what the garden
looked like. You think of the ocean
with its living waters

moving slowly under ice.
You take stock of your life,
how trash laps its edges

while underneath your dreams
invisible gravities
press salt out of your body.

Lose your anchors, one by one.
The only authority
is the weather.

Ask the snow
to teach you patience.
Ask for cover.

No Humble Fruit

I want to be numb
to have winter's chill
force me into dormancy.
I want to hold snow,
push my bare hands
through drifts
up to the elbows
but oranges
are everywhere
piled & glowing,
no humble fruit:
ticking in my palm
a little golden bomb
warm & fragrant
like inside a kiss.

Theobroma Cacao

I place four dark brown hearts on the table,
devour them one by one. They are gone too fast

and I'm still lonely. Some things
can't be sweetened:

as a child I fed my brother raw cocoa
just to watch his face collapse.

He still remembers. A sister's love:
the shock you don't recover from.

Xocoatl laced with lime and chili:
priests with blood-clotted hair

drank as they flung beating hearts to the sun god,
kicked bodies down the pyramid steps.

Blood dries thick, first russet, then umber;
indelible. It anchors the sun in

bitter black seeds. Some things
shouldn't be sweetened –

like that hot brew you gave me
this morning, my love

topped with foam flowing over the lip
of my porcelain cup.

Camellia Garden in October

In waxy shade, a holy
monoculture:

curled into tight green cones,
millions of petals slowly knit.

There are no seasons here,
but precise doses of sun

and water, measured intervals
of sleep and bloom.

California smog and parched earth
halt at the garden gate.

In Eden, days did not lengthen
towards midsummer,

and no one shivered
in a star-cold night;

naked in the damp twilight,
Adam whispered the names of animals

while Eve wiped the dust
from each perfect leaf.

Like the Man Who Fell In Love With Jesus

I want to live in a
body that quakes, I want
someone's fingers to press
marks into my flesh. I want to

open the blue door
of my heart and let
the wolf in. I want
to be in a room
gradually filling
with water. I want to

stand on a corner
and testify, like the man
who fell in love
with Jesus. I want to
breathe and breathe.

I want to know what
the other ninety percent
of my brain is for. I want
to find where my
dreams are filed.

But summer
is going faster than
it came, and every day
I wade through

load after load
of leaves collected
in scarlet puddles
below the shameless trees.

Afternoon in the Shape of a Pear

One hundred pounds
on the kitchen counter,
shoulder-to-shoulder
like sweet, lumpy trolls.
I touch each one, feel
hidden seeds moving
and the hairy tickle
of the blossom-ends.
Something so bland
takes sharpness well:
bleu cheese,
the paring knife.
Perishable flesh
glowing like pearl
leaves sugary grains
under my fingernails.
In its lopsided heart
a lute-shaped crater
hides the worm
who, though blind
knows the importance
of being first.

Irresistible

The bright rich flavor,
the singed edge of fat.
Your teeth
know what they were made for,
your eyes focus, facing forward.
Watch how people eat it:
the lowered knife
the lifted fork, then
the dreamy look.
Wait for the burst of energy,
the power of protein.
Conversation stops, as it should.
This is the story
of soil and horizon
of hoof and broken prairie.
This is the story
of hunger, of slaughter and dust.
There are oceans of grass
and fields of water on your plate.
There is wind whistling
through bone
on your breath.

Shiver

I could die from this,
your hands on my face
your breath like steel.

I am shaped like the Earth.
You are shaped like a weapon.

My edges will never come together
will never develop scar tissue.

I lie down with you
in the high grass where
soldiers fell not so long ago,

the outlines of their bodies
blurred by stealthy moss.

Among the stumbling wounded ghosts
tangled in their woolen coats

desire strafes me.
Where red soil once caked bayonets
I laugh and shiver.

While You Can

Don't be afraid
don't look for signs.
Tomorrow

you will arrive
just after the explosion,
waving your arms through

the light-struck dust.
I'm the ash that coats your tongue,
makes you cough

and cough. No,
I can't stay quiet tonight
on the street made of words.

Soon I will pass through you
like hair through a comb.
Love me while you can,

before the hot air crumbles
like sand; love me like
the black and white sky

spinning.

Seduction of the Bee Queen

My lover wears white.
He lopes into my vision,
arms lethal with gifts.

The smoke of
his breath stuns me:
pores open

all over my body.
He hides his hands
but he is gentle

and I listen
for the soft crinkle

of his suit. I can't say
what happens next.
Sweetness rises from me.

The Redwoods

They suck fog
like whales sift krill;
tattoo my clean car
with bloodred stains
spread from black flowers
too small to see.

On windy nights they sing
of darkness: a need
so strong they fling
branches at my roof
cutting the lights.
There is no blackness

like this, no avoiding
the exchange
of air and trees.
The forest exhales
through trunks in
rows like baleen;

we hang on
for our lives, hands
aching, palms red
with splinters,
layers pressed
into skin, breaking.

This is a Wild Place

On the last day of winter,
my car, filled
with chaff and spare parts,

fits neatly in its painted slot,
a motion box, stopped.
The little junk birds peck at foil,

and I am called away from my body
to forage for my life
out in the open.

When I was eleven
I climbed a huge pine
and had a vision

of flying into the thin
mountain air; my mother called
my name softly, standing on the red earth,

and her voice was a ladder
I climbed down.
I have seen the sky

in late winter, watched clouds
form the ribcage of a fantastic beast,
understanding that

the world is stitched together
from the loosest of tissues – even
concrete, webbed

with faint cracks
leaves nooks
for the smallest seeds.

V

Love Poem with Broken Things

I like to think of him as a small boy, disassembling
the old phonograph his father gave him.

When we moved in together,
he filled our garage with red metal

toolboxes, boxes with drawers
inside of drawers, stuffed with

wrenches of every conceivable size,
drill bits, washers, screws, and nails.

It seemed as if he knew our life ahead
contained a lot of broken things,

and he, for one, was prepared. Back then,
his boxes of tools annoyed me, tripped me,

forced me to park in the driveway.
But now, when I think our life cannot accept

another broken, hopeless thing,
I know that somewhere in the garage

he has a tool that will mend it, tighten it,
wire it or stabilize it, and if he doesn't,

we've learned to let it go with a shrug,
like when he finally admitted he couldn't

put the phonograph back together, and solemnly
handed the screwdriver back to his father.

Early Morning, San Bernardino, 1969

Even then I knew:
my father was waiting
for a message

and we were supposed
to be witnesses.
He could not stop his mind's

wild associations,
but the sky kept its silence,
tar-black and star-smeared.

My brother whimpered,
pinned against the swing set
while Daddy pointed at the heavens,

his *do you see it do you see it*
more and more frantic,
but we didn't see it

wanted our beds
shrank from him
as he trembled, holding

his head with both hands
and the unruly stars
burned out in a desert morning.

I Am No Falconress

> "My mother would be a falconress."
> —Robert Duncan

He was born
with long sharp nails
and when I tried to trim them
blood welled up
and the nurses pursed
their lips.

He hears
the little bells
when he turns
his head.

A young raptor,
my boy:
the intense eye,
the slash from
flesh to bone.
It takes my breath
away, his need
for flight.

My mind follows him
into the blue sky
where I am not
allowed to go.

I am no
falconress, yet
the hood and tether
are there
all the same
and I feel
the claws
at my wrist.

Blindsided

Amid the rap, hip-hop,
house and electronica,
Beethoven's 5th Symphony
has found its way
to my son's iPod.

When Beethoven wrote
the Pastoral, he knew
he was going deaf,
a fact that I think about

when my son
pretends not to hear
a word I say.
During World War II

the first four notes
of the 5th Symphony
ended Netherlands
radio news bulletins.
Beethoven's Bonn birthplace

barely survived
an Allied bomb.
I think about that too
when my son turns
my own words against me

and I feel like a building
where something
significant once happened,
and people still walk by,
stop, nod, and take pictures.

In The Fairytale Forest

In this green and innocent place
swans and deer are not what
they appear to be. The woods

are full of brothers, mirrors,
talking frogs and dwarves.
Trees tangle above, filter

the light, intimate and old.
There's a crack at the edge
of the world where the dark

and comic leak through:
severed finger, soup-bone,
poison apple, circlet of gold –

what is averted? No one here
is anonymous, someone
hoards all weaknesses, all

secrets, how one day long ago
you wished your boy children gone
and in that flash of anger

they became birds and flew
to the forest. There they await
the magic flower shirts

their sister will one day sew
as fast as she can,
while the pyre burns.

Photographs of Elderly Poets

What strange
old children:

the beard-frosted men,
the women

in their windy hair –
reprobate elders

with parabolic ears
and tunnel-black mouths.

Their skulls swell under
stretched and spotted

skin: word-eaters, collectors
of small poisons, their days

and their poems are numbered.
They gaze past us, odd-eyed,

alive in the floating world
even as Death

stands behind them,
filling the empty spaces

in the photographs
with rawboned light.

Glass Lyre Press

exceptional works to replenish the spirit

Glass Lyre Press is an independent literary publisher interested in technically accomplished, stylistically distinct, and original work. Glass Lyre seeks diverse writers that possess a dynamic aesthetic and an ability to emotionally and intellectually engage a wide audience of readers.

Glass Lyre's vision is to connect the world through language and art. We hope to expand the scope of poetry and short fiction for the general reader through exceptionally well-written books, which evoke emotion, provide insight, and resonate with the human spirit.

Poetry Collections
Poetry Chapbooks
Select Short & Flash Fiction
Anthologies

www.GlassLyrePress.com

www.ingramcontent.com/pod-product-compliance
Lightning Source LLC
Chambersburg PA
CBHW021448080526
44588CB00009B/738